MATT CHRISTOPHER®

On the Ice with...
Mario Lemieux

MATT CHRISTOPHER

On the Ice with...

Mario Lemieux

Text by Glenn Stout

 LITTLE, BROWN AND COMPANY

New York • An AOL Time Warner Company

First Edition

Matt Christopher® is a registered trademark of Catherine M. Christopher.

Cover photograph by David E. Klutho

ISBN 0-316-13799-5
LCCN 2002102899

10 9 8 7 6 5 4 3 2 1

COM-MO

Printed in the United States of America

Contents

MATT CHRISTOPHER®

On the Ice with...

Chapter One:

1965–77

The Best

In French, *le mieux* means "the best." Since the day he first stepped on the ice, hockey star Mario Lemieux has lived up to the promise of his name. Despite battles with injury and illness, nothing has stopped him in his quest to be the best hockey player in the world.

Mario was raised in the Canadian province of Quebec. Hockey is Canada's national sport, and in French-speaking Quebec, hockey is more than a game. It is a passion. Most children learn to skate soon after they begin to walk. Every town and neighborhood has an ice-hockey rink. As winter approaches, people can hardly wait for local ponds and lakes to freeze so they can play hockey. Some residents even flood their backyards to create miniature rinks.

Hockey has a long and storied tradition in Canada. The sport became popular in the late 1800s, nowhere more so than in Quebec. The first leagues were formed in 1885, and within ten years Quebec's capital city, Montreal, supported more than one hundred teams. When hockey began to be played professionally around the turn of the century, Montreal was a hotbed of talent. The National Hockey League (NHL) formed in 1917, and the Montreal Canadiens became the sport's reigning dynasty almost from the start.

Mario Lemieux grew up in a working-class neighborhood of Montreal called Ville Emard, only ten minutes away from the Montreal Forum, home of the Canadiens. Mario was born on October 5, 1965, the third son of Jean-Guy Lemieux, a construction worker, and his wife, Pierrette. The three Lemieux boys were very close. Allain, the eldest son, was three years older than Mario. The middle boy, Richard, and Mario were separated by only a year.

There was nothing the boys liked better than playing hockey. By the time Mario first put on skates at the age of three, he already knew the basic rules of the game. He and his brothers pretended that the

Lemieuxs' basement was a hockey rink and would slide about in their stocking feet, using wooden kitchen spoons as hockey sticks and a bottle cap as a puck. They skidded and slid around the columns in the basement, pretending they were defenders, and took aim at their mother's piano, imagining that the space beneath the keyboard was the goal.

Even after Allain began playing organized hockey, and Richard and Mario learned to skate, the boys continued to practice in the basement. Before long, they began using real hockey sticks instead of spoons, and plastic pucks instead of bottle caps.

Their rough play took a toll on the basement's tile ceiling and floor. Each time one of the boys scored, he would thrust his stick in the air in celebration, sometimes piercing one of the tiles. The constant smacking of sticks on the floor as the boys fought for the puck left it scarred and marked. After scoring a goal, they would bang their sticks on the piano.

Fortunately, Pierrette and Jean-Guy didn't mind. Mr. Lemieux was a big hockey fan and was pleased that his sons enjoyed the game so much. He encouraged them to play and just kept replacing tiles and fixing the floor. As the boys grew older, he and his wife were always taking their sons to practices and games. Pierrette and Jean-Guy even carried snow into the house and packed it down on the front hallway, through a door into the dining room, then through the living room and back into the hallway. They left the door open so it would stay cold and the boys could skate through the house! Neighbors and relatives thought the Lemieuxs were nuts, but as Pierrette said later, "It was easy to raise kids here. There was always happiness."

Mario learned to skate with other neighborhood kids and his many cousins on an outdoor rink behind a nearby church. He took to the ice immediately. Before he began attending school, the whole neighborhood was already talking about how well he could skate. "They all said, 'Look at this little guy, look at him go, look at him skate!'" Pierrette recalled.

Mario's early career wasn't restricted to pickup games of hockey. There were also organized leagues for kids. Youth hockey in Canada is very popular. Leagues are organized around age groups, so players compete against others of similar skills. When

Mario was growing up, a player had to be nine years old to be eligible to play. Teams of young players compete for provincial titles and sometimes travel long distances. Teenage hockey players are also subject to a draft to play in the highly competitive junior leagues. They often move away from home and even quit school in order to further their hockey careers.

When Mario was six years old, his brother Allain was playing for a Pee Wee league hockey team of nine- and ten-year-olds. One afternoon, they were playing a practice game when the coach motioned for Mario to come down from the stands. He had noticed the young boy skating around before the game and asked him if he'd like to play.

Mario jumped at the chance. He'd never played in a real game before. Although he was three or four years younger than everyone else, he wasn't intimidated. Mario was already as big as kids several years older.

He played as if he had been practicing with the team all year. He'd only been on the ice a few minutes before he scored a goal, and a few minutes later he made a nice pass and collected an assist.

Mario could hardly wait until he was old enough to join Pee Wee hockey. Over the next few years, he played pickup hockey whenever he could, usually against older boys. Yet, even then, he was often the best player on the ice.

When he turned nine, he joined the Ville Emard Hurricanes, known as the Black Machine in reference to the color of their jerseys. The Hurricanes were a legend in Pee Wee league hockey in the Montreal area. They were usually one of the best teams.

Mario's teammates on the Hurricanes included two future NHL hockey players, J. J. Daigneault and Sylvain Cote, who later became a first-round draft pick in the NHL. Despite being surrounded by such talent, Mario stood out.

His size, even then, was intimidating. When Mario had the puck it was almost impossible to take it away. Other players feared being checked by Mario. Although he played by the rules, he was already tough and strong. He had a powerful shot, and his stickhandling ability was better than that of most other players.

But what made Mario stand out most were his vision and hockey instincts. He played as if he had eyes in the back of his head and seemed able to sense what was going to happen before it did. He would make a blind pass an instant before a player broke clear or swoop in the opposite direction just as an opponent moved in from behind. The combination of his skills made him a unique player. He did more than score; he made his entire team better.

Mario soon developed a reputation as one of the best young players in Quebec. When the Hurricanes competed in the provincial Pee Wee league tournament and played throughout Quebec, fans turned out in droves to see him play, immediately picking out the young boy in the Number 12 jersey who towered over most of the other players.

Canadian fans take hockey very seriously, even youth hockey. Mario would often be greeted with jeers from the supporters of the opposing team. Steve Finn, who later played in the NHL, played against Lemieux in the tournament, and later told a reporter, "Already, he had a big reputation. Everyone was talking about him." Adult spectators sometimes greeted Mario with obscenities. Some people even threw things at him and spat on him as he skated past.

Mario led the Hurricanes to the provincial championship. As he grew older and moved up to leagues for older kids, Montreal newspaper reporters often found themselves writing about the young star. Mario was the best player on every team he played on, and he usually made his team the best in the league.

Scotty Bowman, a former coach of the Montreal Canadiens, kept seeing Mario's name in the newspaper. He was intrigued by the boy's last name — "the best" — and decided to see for himself if this boy was as good as everyone claimed he was. One day, when Mario was twelve years old, Bowman quietly sat in the back of an arena and watched him play. He saw a special player. It was almost as if Mario were playing a different game from the other boys on the ice.

Nearly a decade earlier Wayne Gretzky, a young player in the Toronto area, had been a youth-hockey prodigy. He had gone on to be a star in junior hockey and turned pro at age seventeen, joining a new pro league, the World Hockey Association. When the league folded a year later, his team, the Edmonton Oilers, joined the long-established National Hockey League. At age eighteen, Gretzky tied for the NHL scoring title and won the MVP award, the Hart Trophy. Although he was still in his twenties, many people considered Gretzky the best hockey player ever. But after seeing Mario, Bowman was convinced that he was just as special as Wayne Gretzky.

Bowman couldn't contain his enthusiasm. He told a reporter, "I have seen a young man named Mario Lemieux play hockey. He will be a future star in the NHL."

Such a ringing endorsement got everyone's attention. Wayne Gretzky's agent, Bob Perno, read the story and decided that he, too, just had to see this young man named Mario Lemieux.

Perno had a reaction similar to Bowman's. "I just fell in love with him," he recalled. "Just fell in love." When he returned home, he called a business partner and said, "This guy is good."

When his partner asked just how good he was, Perno didn't hesitate. "This guy is another Wayne," he said. "Only bigger."

Although Perno was speaking about Lemieux's size, those words also rang true in regard to Mario's potential. Over the next few years, the hockey world would anxiously watch to see if Mario Lemieux would fulfill his promise.

Chapter Two:

1978–84

Major Decisions

In the United States, most hockey players compete in high school and college before turning professional. But in Canada, hockey is organized differently. After youth hockey, the best young Canadian players move on to compete in junior hockey, highly competitive leagues primarily for teenagers. Junior hockey is divided into several divisions for players of varying skill levels. Major Junior is the top classification, followed by Junior A, B, and C. The three Major Junior leagues — the Western Hockey League (WHL), the Ontario Hockey League (OHL), and the Quebec Major Junior Hockey League (QMJHL) — are known collectively as the Canadian Hockey League (CHL). This league of approximately fifty teams is only one step below professional hockey. The National Hockey League considers the Major

Junior leagues as breeding grounds for talent. The CHL has even adopted the slogan "Official Supplier to the National Hockey League."

Only the best young players are selected to play Major Junior hockey. The workload is intense. Each team plays a lengthy schedule that includes a lot of travel and practices nearly every day. Many players move away from home to play, and some even quit school. Although the players aren't paid, some Major Junior games attract big crowds of several thousand fans. The players become local celebrities.

Although most Major Junior hockey players are at least seventeen years old, on rare occasions players a year or two younger are allowed to play. Wayne Gretzky, for instance, played in Major Junior hockey at age fifteen.

The Lemieux family already knew all about Major Junior hockey. Beginning in 1978, Mario's brother Allain played three seasons for the Chicoutimi Saqueneens and the Trois-Rivieres Draveurs. At the end of the 1980–81 season, he made the QMJHL second-team All-Star squad. His hard work paid off. He was drafted by the NHL's St. Louis Blues and became a professional.

Mario Lemieux began his Major Junior career at age sixteen, joining the Montreal-based Laval Voisins, also known as the Titans. He and his family were immediately faced with an important decision.

Mario was already considered a top professional prospect. To enhance his chances of a pro career, Mario's parents agreed to allow him to drop out of tenth grade. While they thought they might be criticized for making such a decision, they knew Mario would always be able to go back to school. For the time being, they decided that hockey was more important.

And Mario still promised to work hard, on and off the ice. While his classmates trudged off to school, Mario went to the nearby rink behind the church and worked out alone, skating for as many as four hours a day, trying to improve.

He also took a crash course in English. In Quebec, the French language is dominant. Very few people speak English. Mario's parents didn't speak English well, and except for a few words and phrases, neither did Mario.

Mario was already looking ahead. He knew that if he became a professional hockey player he might have to play in the United States. If he didn't speak English, he'd have a hard time communicating. And even if he remained in Quebec, or was drafted by a Canadian team, he would have to be able to speak with all his teammates and answer questions from the English-speaking press.

But once the season started, his focus turned back to hockey. In recent years, the Voisins hadn't been very successful. From the first time Mario skated onto the ice, though, Laval became one of the best teams in the league.

Mario made it clear to everyone that his goal was not only to play professional hockey, but also to live up to his name, to become the best. Wayne Gretzky wore the number 99, so Lemieux decided to wear the Number 66 — 99 upside down. Although he later said, "I didn't want to be compared to Gretzky," such comparisons were inevitable, particularly when fans saw him play.

He already stood more than six feet tall, towering over many of his teammates. Like Gretzky, Mario played center, a position that took advantage of both his scoring ability and his playmaking and passing skills. A top-notch center makes his linemates, the two wingers that play on his line, much better. A talented center can make a team better overnight.

Even though he was one of the youngest players in the league, he was already one of the best. In his first season, Mario worked hard to fit in, usually looking to pass before he shot. Although he scored only 30 goals in 64 games, he picked up 66 assists, making passes that helped his teammates score. In hockey, a player's stats include a total point value. This value is the number of goals plus the number of assists. Mario had a total of 96 points his first season. Mario's contributions helped Laval improve from 21 wins in the 1980–81 season to finish the 1981–82 season 30–33 with 1 tie, for 61 points. In hockey leagues, each win earns a team 2 points and a tie is worth only 1.

Professional scouts didn't take long to conclude that Mario was every bit as good as his reputation. The Montreal Canadiens decided to do everything they could to ensure that Lemieux would one day become a member of their team.

Mario wouldn't be eligible for the draft until he turned eighteen at the conclusion of the 1983–84 season. Then, the team with the worst record in the league would have the right to make the first pick in the draft. The Hartford Whalers were one of the worst teams in the NHL, and the Canadiens, the most successful team, thought the Whalers had a good chance of finishing last in 1984.

So the Canadiens made a trade with the Whalers that included the option of switching draft picks with them. If the Whalers finished last, the Canadiens planned to select Mario with the first pick of the draft.

Mario's progress continued in the 1982–83 season. He began to shoot more often, and he finished with 84 goals and 100 assists in 66 games. The Voisins were one of the top teams in the CHL, finishing the season 53–17.

But it was in his final season of Major Junior hockey that Mario truly blossomed. No one, not even Wayne Gretzky, had ever had a season in the CHL like Mario Lemieux did in 1983–84. He was a scoring machine, averaging nearly 2 goals a game, finishing with 133 goals and 149 assists in only 70 games. At one point Mario scored in 52 consecutive games. Laval finished in first place with a record of 54–16 and made it to the Memorial Cup, the CHL championship series. Although they lost in the finals, Mario played well. One observer recalled, "I saw him take the puck twice and go right through the whole team" before scoring.

NHL scouts salivated at the prospect of obtaining Lemieux. He now stood six feet four inches tall and weighed more than 200 pounds, a rare blend of size, speed, and strength. Wayne Gretzky, for all his talent, was small for a hockey player, barely six feet tall. Despite his skill, he couldn't play a physical style of hockey. Mario could. He was equally adept at skating both through the opposition and around them. Fans loved his flair, too. Although he was soft-spoken off the ice, he was a natural showman in the rink. After scoring a goal, Lemieux would drop to his knees and pump his arms in the air, a wide smile on his face. Already, kids throughout Quebec were imitating Mario. He was the kind of player you could build a team around.

The only questions about him concerned his work ethic. As one hockey insider later observed, "He was so superior to the players he was playing that it took away from his game." Despite all the points he scored, there were times when Lemieux seemed to coast on the ice, particularly on defense. In some instances, Mario claimed that he coasted on purpose. "I'll wait until I see a guy's getting tired, then I'll make my move," he said. But he also admitted, "Maybe it gave some people the wrong idea. . . . I'm the type of player who will work when I have to work."

Meanwhile, more NHL teams were scheming to figure out some way to acquire him. As the NHL season progressed, it became clear that either the New Jersey Devils or the Pittsburgh Penguins would finish with the worst record in the league. A number of teams, including the Canadiens, had standing trade offers for the number-one draft pick. The Minnesota North Stars were even prepared to offer their entire draft — all twelve picks — to the team that won the right to draft Mario.

But both Pittsburgh and New Jersey were determined to keep the pick if either finished last. Each turned down numerous trade offers. In fact, as the season wound down, some charged that the two clubs were trying to lose on purpose just to make certain they would be able to pick Mario.

The Penguins were particularly eager. Late in the

season, they traded their best player, defenseman Randy Carlyle, to the Winnipeg Jets for a draft pick and player to be named later. Then, with only four games remaining in the regular season, they sent their best goalkeeper down to the minor leagues. His replacement gave up 24 goals in only 4 games. The Penguins lost all 4, and finished the season with 6 straight losses to end the year in last place, 3 points behind New Jersey, winning the rights to select Mario.

Pittsburgh and the rest of the NHL could hardly wait.

Chapter Three:
1984

The Savior

The Penguins had watched Mario closely in the Major Juniors. As June 9, 1984, the date of the NHL draft, approached, other NHL clubs continued to try to pry the draft pick away from the Penguins.

But Penguin owner Eddie DeBartolo and general manager Eddie Johnston held firm, even turning down an offer from the Quebec Nordiques of the three Stastny brothers, all solid starters in the NHL. In the past, the Penguins had often traded their top draft picks for veterans, usually with disastrous results. This time, they were determined to make Mario a Penguin. As Johnston said, of all the players available in the draft, Mario "was the only franchise player." Penguin coach Bob Berry said simply, "No one who's come out of junior hockey has ever shown as much potential as Mario — ever."

And no team in the NHL was in more need of a franchise player than the Pittsburgh Penguins. While Pittsburgh had briefly supported an NHL franchise in the 1920s, the Pittsburgh Pirates, the franchise soon moved and left the league. In the 1930s, pro hockey returned to Pittsburgh when the Hornets were created and joined the American Hockey League, hockey's most successful minor league. The Hornets attracted a small but rabid following, and when the NHL decided to expand in 1967, Pittsburgh was awarded a franchise, adopting the nickname Penguins.

But the Penguins had a hard time winning. After the 1974–75 season, the team went bankrupt and almost folded before being sold. After making the playoffs and advancing to the division finals in 1981–82, the franchise went into a tailspin, finishing last in the Patrick Division. In the 1983–84 season, the Penguins averaged fewer than seven thousand fans, less than half the capacity of the Civic Arena, known in Pittsburgh as the Igloo. Not a single game was a sellout.

Although Mario had said, "I just want to play in the NHL. I want to play for whoever drafts me," as

21

draft day approached he began to send out a mixed message. The Penguins began negotiating with Lemieux and his agent before the draft, and the two sides were deadlocked.

Some thought that Mario and his agent were trying to force the Penguins to trade the number-one pick to a better team, but the Pittsburgh franchise continued to reject the idea. Everyone in Pittsburgh wanted Mario to become a Penguin. The Penguins even broadcast the draft, held in the Montreal Forum, back to Pittsburgh. More than 3,000 fans, almost half of their usual crowd for a game, showed up at the Igloo to watch the proceedings on closed-circuit television.

Penguin general manager Eddie Johnston knew this was a historic occasion and played the moment for all it was worth. He stepped up to the microphone, paused dramatically, and then spoke.

"*Mesdames et messieurs* (Ladies and gentlemen)," he said in French, acknowledging Lemieux's background, "the Pittsburgh Penguins are proud to select first overall *dans les Voisins de Laval* (from the Laval Voisins), *Numéro Soixante-six, le centre* (Number Sixty-six, center), Mario Lemieux!" The Igloo erupted with cheers and applause.

Mario and his agent reluctantly approached the podium. Mario refused to shake Johnston's hand and wouldn't pose in a Penguin jersey. He was upset over the negotiations and in a press conference afterward said, "Pittsburgh doesn't want me bad enough."

The Penguins were embarrassed and wondered if they'd made a mistake. And back in Pittsburgh, where the unemployment rate was nearly 20 percent, Penguin fans were put off. They thought Mario was acting like a jerk.

Yet it was all part of a negotiating ploy designed by Mario's agent. Only a few weeks later, everyone was smiling when the two sides came to an agreement. Mario signed a two-year contract for $600,000, including a $150,000 signing bonus. Lemieux was finally a professional and a Penguin.

But he was only eighteen years old, moving to a new city, in a new country, with more money than he knew what to do with. Although his hockey skills were ready for the NHL, he wasn't mature enough to deal with life as a professional athlete.

The Penguins understood that. They wanted to make sure that Mario didn't get into trouble or become homesick. A decade earlier, Pierre Larouche had joined the Penguins at age eighteen. Many hockey observers thought his progress had been delayed because he had a hard time adjusting to being on his own. The Penguins hadn't given him much direction, and he spent too much time partying with his older teammates. Although he still became a fine player, Larouche never fulfilled his potential in Pittsburgh.

General manager Eddie Johnston had been in professional hockey for decades. As a member of the Boston Bruins in the 1960s, he saw how the Bruins had taken care of their phenom Bobby Orr, and Johnston was determined to help Lemieux in the same way.

He was friends with Tom and Nancy Mathews, a couple with three hockey-playing sons, the last of which had just left home to go to college. Johnston asked them if they would consider letting Lemieux move in and acting as his surrogate family while he adjusted to life in the NHL. The Mathews welcomed him, and after meeting them, Lemieux quickly agreed to the arrangement. Lemieux's parents visited the Mathews, and the two families discovered they had a lot in common. As Nancy Mathews later said, "When you're a mother, you take one look at that face and realize that he's shy and in another country, and you just want to step in and help."

Lemieux fit right in. He helped with chores around the house, played with the family dog, and, when the Mathews' sons came home to visit, made friends. Living with the Mathews made the adjustment to professional hockey easier. He was able to concentrate on playing without worrying about anything. The Mathews took care of him.

When Lemieux took the ice at the Penguins' first practice, Pittsburgh fans quickly embraced him. The whole city was excited. Preseason practices had always been free and open to the public, but few fans bothered to attend. Lemieux changed all that. Hundreds of fans showed up every day, and the Penguins soon began charging $1 admission.

Lemieux didn't disappoint the fans. On September 20, during his first shift in the Penguins' first intersquad scrimmage, Lemieux gave them something to remember.

His team had the puck, and Lemieux went charging down the ice. A teammate hit him with a pass in the slot, the area between the goal and the face-off circle. As a defenseman charged toward him, Lemieux tapped the puck between the defender's skates, avoided the charge like a matador sidestepping a bull, retrieved the puck, and swept a wrist shot into the net past the startled goalkeeper. Goal!

The crowd erupted. It wasn't just a good goal — it was a great goal. One fan screamed, "Our savior has arrived!" Lemieux appeared to be as good as advertised. For the next hour, he kept the crowd buzzing as he skated through the opposition with ease, making passes so good that they often caught his teammates by surprise. One member of the Penguins' front office called his performance scary, saying, "He did things that only Gretzky can do. That's what's scary: to think that there might be another one." Penguin fans could hardly wait for the start of the season and bought tickets by the handful.

He continued to impress in the exhibition season

and averaged 2 points a game. Already, the opposition was running out of ways to describe him, comparing him not only to Gretzky but also to other NHL greats like Phil Esposito and Bobby Orr. But it was still the exhibition season. When the regular season began, Lemieux was certain to be tested.

The Penguins opened the season on the road on October 11, 1984, facing the rough-and-tough Boston Bruins at the famous Boston Garden. The Bruins had a well-deserved reputation as one of the most physical teams in the league, and the crowd at the Garden was known for giving young players a hard time. Lemieux's first game promised to be a challenge.

On Mario's very first shift, Bruins star defenseman Ray Bourque had the puck at the right point, just inside the blue line near the boards. Lemieux moved in to challenge him. As Bourque described it later, "I tried to pass the puck between his stick and his skate. It hit his skate and he was gone."

The puck deflected off the boards. Lemieux gathered it in and took off like a rocket. Before Bourque even had a chance to react, Lemieux was free and swept past on a breakaway. All he saw before him were clear ice and Bruins All-Star goalkeeper Pete Peeters.

Lemieux charged down the ice, keeping the puck on his stick, then skated toward the goalmouth. Peeters crouched, watching him closely, expecting the rookie to be anxious and try to blast a shot past him. "I just stood there and forced him to make a move," said Peeters later. "And he made his move."

Mario Lemieux was a rookie in name only. He deftly skated across the goal, switched the puck from his forehand to his backhand, and beat the sprawling goalie. He had scored only 2:59 into the game!

Lemieux fell to his knee and raised his stick as his teammates skated by, tapping him in celebration. One goal, his first, was already in the books. Many more would soon follow.

It didn't take long for the Bruins to realize that if they wanted to stop the Penguins, they had to stop Lemieux. For much of the remainder of the game they checked him closely, sometimes using more than one defender to cover him. Although he later added an assist, and the Penguins took a 3–1 lead,

NHL. They had heard about Lemieux's spectacular goal against Boston and were determined to shut him down. Montreal center Guy Charbonneau and his linemates, Bob Gainey and Chris Nilan, focused their efforts on Lemieux and held him to only two shots. Although Lemieux picked up an assist with a nifty pass, the Canadiens won 4–3.

"There was a lot of pressure because all my family was there, and most of the people were there to watch me. It was tough," admitted Lemieux later. "The team didn't play well, so it was tough for me to play well."

After the game, he still answered every question and found time to attend a reception. But after two games on the road, he was looking forward to making his debut in Pittsburgh.

Lemieux was fitting in well with his teammates. Already, they looked to him as a leader. Despite his reputation and his big contract, he didn't act like a big star. His teammates treated him like any other rookie. That included making him the butt of their practical jokes.

On the flight from Montreal to Pittsburgh, Lemieux fell asleep with his head nodding forward.

As he napped beneath his baseball cap, his team-mates carefully applied a mound of shaving cream to the brim of his cap. When he awoke, he reached up to grab his cap and knocked the tower of shaving cream into his lap! But Lemieux didn't get angry. He laughed along with his teammates. The prank was their way of telling him that he belonged.

The Penguins promoted his first appearance in Pittsburgh in a regular season game as the Lemieux Debut on October 17. Despite a terrible storm raging outside, the Igloo was packed to the rafters with a capacity crowd of 15,714. Lemieux didn't disappoint them.

The crowd roared when he took the ice for pregame warm-ups and kept up the din through the introductions. Just moments after the opening face-off, they got what they wanted.

Lemieux took the puck and cut past Vancouver Canucks defenseman Doug Halward outside the visitors' blue line, then skated down the left-wing boards. As the Canucks moved toward him, he fired a perfect pass to teammate Doug Skedden, who buried the puck into the goal. Only eighteen seconds into the game, the Penguins led 1–0. The crowd started chanting, "MAR-I-O! MAR-I-O!"

In the NHL, any talented offensive player soon becomes a target. The opposition tends to treat such players roughly, grabbing at them, throwing elbows, and doing anything possible to slow them down and take them out of their game. While such rough play is illegal, it is impossible for the referees to see every infraction. As long as it doesn't get out of hand, rough play is part of professional hockey.

The Canucks decided to test Lemieux. They hoped to intimidate him and make him change his style of play. Canuck Gary Lupul speared Lemieux with the butt end of his stick. Lemieux let the infraction go.

But a few minutes later, Lupul speared him again. Lemieux knew that if he didn't respond, he might get a reputation for being soft, for allowing other players to take advantage of him. If that happened, he would be the subject of rough play at every opportunity. He had to demonstrate that he would and could defend himself when necessary.

Lemieux reached out and grabbed Lupul, and the

two scuffled. Referees separated the two players, but Lemieux got his message across. If he had to, he was willing to respond to rough play. And at six foot four and more than two hundred pounds, he was well equipped to do so.

Pittsburgh won the Lemieux Debut 4–3. In his first 3 games, he had scored 1 goal and collected 3 assists. Eddie Johnston spoke for everyone when he said, "He's going to be a good player in this league for a long time."

Other teams in the NHL took notice of Lemieux's quick start. From the moment Lemieux skated onto the ice, he discovered he was the focus of the opposition's defense. While he initially found it difficult to score goals, his passing and playmaking skills still made him an offensive force. When the defense collapsed around him, it usually meant that one or more of his teammates were free. Lemieux wisely passed off and gave his teammates opportunities to score.

He didn't score his second NHL goal until his fourteenth game, an overtime winner versus Winnipeg. That goal seemed to break the ice, and he began scoring with regularity. As one of his teammates commented later, "He's shooting the puck more. In the beginning, he was always looking for his wingers. He'd make great plays, get in position, and then pass the puck. He's so unselfish."

While the Penguins weren't yet one of the best teams in the league, with Lemieux on the ice they weren't pushovers anymore. In the past, teams had looked forward to playing the Penguins, expecting to pick up a win and add 2 easy points to their team total. Now they had to fight and scrap to beat them.

Moreover, Lemieux made the Penguins an instant box-office success. Average attendance at the Igloo soared to more than ten thousand fans a game. And whenever the Penguins asked Lemieux to make a promotional appearance, signing autographs or giving a short speech, he drew huge crowds. When the Penguins played on the road, they drew larger crowds than ever before.

Lemieux was selected to the All-Star team, and after scoring two goals and collecting an assist in the game, he was named the All-Star MVP. Lemieux was clearly the best rookie in the league and already one of the best players. In the opinion of many hockey observers, he was surpassing the expectations that accompanied his entry into the league.

But that success came with a price. As the season wore on, Lemieux found himself becoming the target of more and more rough play. He realized that being a target was, in a sense, a badge of honor, a sign of just how big a threat he had become on the ice. Yet during the second half of the season, Lemieux was getting attacked in almost every game. It was hard for him not to get frustrated.

As he put it, he realized that it wasn't his "job to fight, to sit in the penalty box for five or seven minutes." He even suffered a concussion when Winnipeg Jets Jim Kyte sucker punched him, an act that earned Kyte a five-game suspension.

A few days later, the Penguins provided Lemieux with some protection. They picked up Wally Weir, a so-called enforcer, a hockey player known as much for his fighting skills as for his on-ice finesse. The move sent a message to the other teams. If they continued to beat up on Lemieux, Weir would make them pay for it.

While Lemieux continued to play well, and the Penguins were much improved, it was their misfortune to play in the Patrick Division, one of the NHL's toughest divisions. The Penguins needed to finish fourth in the six-team division in order to make the playoffs, but the division included several of the league's best teams. The Philadelphia Flyers, Washington Capitals, New York Islanders, and New York Rangers were all tough, and the New Jersey Devils were improving. Although the Penguins challenged for a playoff spot into February, they slumped toward the end of the season and still finished last in the division with 53 points, 1 point behind New Jersey and 9 points short of the playoffs. Still, that was an improvement of 15 points and 8 wins from the previous season. The Penguins planned to build the team around Lemieux and knew it might take a while to acquire enough other good players to become a playoff team.

Lemieux scored an even 100 points in the season with 43 goals and 57 assists, the highest scorer on the team. To no one's surprise, at the end of the season Lemieux won the prestigious Calder Memorial Trophy, which was awarded annually to the league's best rookie.

But the best part of the year was that it was over. Mario Lemieux wasn't a rookie anymore.

Chapter Five:
1985-88

O Canada

After the season, Lemieux was asked to play for the Canadian team in the World and European championships, an international tournament. He was joined on the squad by other Canadian NHL stars, including Wayne Gretzky. Although Canada finished second to the Soviet Union, Lemieux held his own in the tournament, scoring 10 points in 9 games.

Expectations for Lemieux were high at the beginning of the 1985–86 season.

As his second season began, Lemieux felt more comfortable in Pittsburgh. He moved into his own apartment and began to take on more responsibility both on and off the ice.

Led by Lemieux, the Penguins kept improving. Lemieux soon proved that his success in his rookie season was no fluke. In midseason, with the Penguins challenging for a playoff spot and Lemieux second in the NHL in scoring to Wayne Gretzky, the Penguins tore up his contract and signed him to a five-year deal worth $650,000 a year. Attendance at the Igloo had continued to increase. Before Lemieux arrived in Pittsburgh, there had been talk that the franchise might have to move. Now the Penguin franchise was stable and getting stronger. Eddie Johnston summed up everyone's feelings when he said, "He means just about everything to us."

Lemieux's game was improving, too, particularly on the defensive end. In junior hockey, Lemieux had rarely been called upon to play defense. But in the NHL, the ability to play defense was just as important as the ability to score. Penguin coach Bob Berry taught Lemieux to use his size and strength to thwart the opposition.

But offense was still the centerpiece of Lemieux's game. Most opponents tried to play him aggressively, and Lemieux became adept at using their aggressiveness to his advantage.

"If you go at Mario like a madman," said Boston

Bruins star defenseman Ray Bourque, "he'll make you look like an idiot. He just holds the puck out there on his forehand and dares you to commit yourself. If you do, he slips it past you." If a defender gives Lemieux some room, admitted Bourque, Lemieux "has time to make the play."

Increased expectations for Lemieux led to some impatience from the press, the fans, and his own teammates. Even though he scored 141 points with 48 goals and 93 assists, the Penguins were edged out of the last playoff spot on the last day of the season. Some blamed Mario for the team's failure.

He received even more criticism during the off-season when he turned down an opportunity to represent Canada in the World and European Championships. But Lemieux had been playing hockey almost nonstop his entire life. He wanted to take some time off. His girlfriend, Nathalie, lived in Montreal, and Lemieux wanted to spend time with her and his family.

Some people thought Lemieux was becoming stuck-up as he made fewer public appearances and spoke to the press less often. In truth, he was really quite shy. He didn't like being the center of attention and always believed that the way he played the game would do his talking for him.

But during the off-season, Lemieux fell into some bad habits. He didn't train very much and got out of shape. He started smoking, too, which hurt his stamina. And at age twenty-one, he began spending time out on the town, partying. Although he wasn't out of control, hockey wasn't quite as important as it once had been. Thus far, Lemieux had succeeded because of his size and natural ability. He hadn't had to work very hard to be one of the best players in hockey.

It cost him during the 1986–87 season. He was still one of the better players in the game even though he missed some time with injuries and his scoring output slumped. He scored 54 goals, but his assist total dropped to 53 and he scored only 107 points for the season. For most players, that would have been a spectacular season. But for Lemieux, it represented a step backward. Moreover, the Penguins, after improving dramatically in his first two seasons and winning their first 7 games of the 1986–87 season, fell back and finished with only 30 wins, fifth in the division again. They failed to make the playoffs. Coach Bob Berry was fired at the end of the season and replaced by Pierre Creamer.

It wasn't all Lemieux's fault, because the Penguins really didn't have much talent, and it was unfair to expect Lemieux to carry the team on his back the entire season. Even so, hockey people began to whisper that Lemieux, for all his skills, simply wasn't a winner. Unlike Wayne Gretzky, they didn't think he wanted to work hard enough to succeed.

Nevertheless, Lemieux was asked to try out for the Canadian team in the 1987 Canada Cup, an international tournament that consisted of a round-robin tournament against the five best national hockey teams. The Cup was a great source of pride in Canada, as important as the Olympics. Although Canada won the inaugural Cup in 1976, they lost to the Soviet Union in the second Cup in 1981. The whole country had been embarrassed. Even though Canada recaptured the Cup in 1984, they were expected to repeat as champions in 1987.

Training camp began even as the Stanley Cup playoffs continued. It was a unique experience for Lemieux — he hadn't tried out for a team in years.

But with thirty-four players trying out for only twenty-three roster spots, Lemieux's place on the team was anything but certain, particularly after his disappointing regular season.

Wayne Gretzky joined the team near the end of camp, after leading his Edmonton Oilers to the Stanley Cup championship. At the end of a long and grueling season, it would have been understandable if Gretzky had taken it easy at training camp. Instead, he set the tone.

Lemieux was amazed at how hard Gretzky worked. Although Gretzky had complained earlier in the year about the timing of the Canada Cup, which would give him virtually no time off between the end of the playoffs and the beginning of the 1987–88 season, he was the hardest worker in camp.

Gretzky inspired Lemieux to work harder in practice. During intersquad scrimmages, he sometimes had to play opposite Gretzky. He didn't want to be embarrassed by the best player in the game. As Lemieux said later, "Every shift Wayne tried to do the impossible." Lemieux tried to match his intensity.

In the first round of the tournament, each team

played every other team. The four teams with the most points then advanced to the semifinals. The winners of the one-game semifinals would then play a best-of-three series for the Cup. Although Canada made it through the round-robin portion of the tournament undefeated, they hadn't played particularly well, tying Czechoslovakia in their first game and the Soviet Union in their final. Lemieux, however, had impressed everyone with his play, scoring a hat trick (3 goals) in a 3–2 win over Finland.

Since Lemieux and Gretzky both played center, they were only on the ice at the same time during four-on-fours or power plays, when Lemieux played right forward or wing. When one reporter asked coach Mike Keenan why he didn't play the two together all the time, the coach responded, "It would be counterproductive." He thought it was important to keep each man fresh and in the middle on his own line.

The Soviet Union defeated Sweden to reach the finals. Canada played Czechoslovakia for the right to play the Soviets.

Czechoslovakia, keyed by the play of goalie Dominik Hasek, held a 2–0 lead late in the game. It appeared as if Canada wouldn't even reach the finals. The whole country would be embarrassed.

But Dale Hawerchuck slipped a goal past Hasek, then Lemieux took over. In a two-minute span, he scored twice, and the Canadians held on to win 3–2. The two best teams in hockey would square off for the Cup.

By then, Coach Keenan had changed his mind about putting Lemieux and Gretzky on the ice together. He knew that the powerful Soviet team, which had played together for years, was likely to score some goals. Although the Canadian team was more talented, the simple fact that they hadn't played together as a team for very long gave the Soviets a huge advantage.

Yet, Lemieux and Gretzky played as if they had skated together for years. Keenan thought that putting them on the ice at the same time would give his team a chance to outscore the Russians.

The first game was a classic. Each team battled for every goal, but the Soviets won 6–5 in overtime. Canada couldn't afford another loss.

In the second game, the Canadians jumped out

at the beginning of the game to a 3–1 lead. But the Soviets came back to tie the game at 4–4. A Lemieux goal put Canada ahead again, but the Soviets tied the score just before the end of regulation play. The game entered overtime. Both teams would play extra twenty-minute periods until someone scored.

The first overtime ended scoreless. The Canadians and the Soviets were exhausted, but neither team would give in.

Lemieux, however, still felt fresh. The example set by Gretzky during training had paid off. Mario was in the best shape of his life. He later said that he had a premonition and had visualized himself scoring the winning goal. Ten minutes into the second overtime, he received his opportunity.

The task of covering both Gretzky and Lemieux had given the Soviets trouble. All the extra energy they exerted had worn them down.

From the high slot, a Canadian defender passed the puck to Gretzky, who was positioned to the left of the Russian goal. Lemieux sensed the pass before it even took place and slashed into the crease. As soon as the puck reached Gretzky's stick, he sent a pass to Lemieux on the fly. He took it in stride and snapped it past the startled Soviet goalkeeper.

Score! Lemieux collapsed to his knees and was surrounded by his teammates. The next game would decide the Cup.

The finale unfolded much like Game Two, only this time it was the Soviets who took the early advantage, leading after the first period 4–2. In the locker room between periods, however, Coach Keenan sensed that his team hadn't given up. "The mood in the locker room," he said later, "was that we were going to participate in the greatest comeback in the history of the game." The two greatest players in hockey, Numbers 99 and 66, Gretzky and Lemieux, would key that comeback.

Canada fought back to tie the score 5–5, and the clock ticked down toward the end of regulation play. But with only 1:26 left to play, another perfect pass by Gretzky found Lemieux. He fired it into the net. Goal!

A few moments later, the game ended. Canada had won, and Mario Lemieux was a national hero. The 1987–88 NHL season began only a few weeks later. Lemieux had never felt more prepared. Playing with Gretzky gave him a sense of just how good he could be. He was determined to have his best season ever.

His teammates immediately noticed the change. Lemieux had matured. Linemate and forward Phil Bourque later remarked that "he was a different person" after the Canada Cup. Lemieux seemed to realize that it was time to get serious and fulfill his potential.

Lemieux played the best hockey of his young career. Early in the season, the Penguins traded for veteran defenseman Paul Coffey of the Edmonton Oilers. Coffey helped slow down Pittsburgh opponents and also provided another consistent scoring threat. The other teams had difficulty covering both Lemieux and Coffey at the same time. At the season's end, Lemieux led the league in goals with 70 and had 98 assists.

He edged out Wayne Gretzky to win the Art Ross Trophy, an award given to the league's lead scorer. His performance also earned him the Hart Trophy, the NHL's MVP award, and he was named to the first team of the All-Star squad. The Penguins, after a slow start, recovered, winning 11 of their last 15 games to finish with their best season in a decade, ending the year above .500 at 36–35–9 for 81 points.

In most seasons, that record would have been enough to put the Penguins in the playoffs. But in 1987–88, the Patrick Division race was the closest in NHL history. The New York Islanders won the division with 88 points, while the Capitals and Flyers tied for second with 85. The Devils and Rangers tied for third place with 82 points. Though they had finished only 7 points out of first place, the Penguins wound up last in the division and failed to make the playoffs.

Despite his personal accomplishments, Mario Lemieux knew that until he led his team into the playoffs and captured the Stanley Cup, his career would be incomplete. Over the next few seasons, that would be his goal.

Chapter Six:
1988-90

Slipping Back

Pittsburgh hockey fans were beginning to run out of patience. Although they loved watching Lemieux play, they wanted the Penguins to become a championship team. They hadn't qualified for the playoffs since 1981. Sixteen of the twenty-one teams in the NHL at the time qualified for postseason play each year, and most Pittsburgh fans thought the Penguins should make the playoffs every year. So did Lemieux and team owner Eddie DeBartolo.

But one or two players don't make a team. That had been Pittsburgh's problem. Apart from Lemieux and now Coffey, the Penguins didn't really have a big star. One of Lemieux's teammates even went so far as to call Lemieux "sixty to seventy percent of the offense." When Lemieux didn't score, the Penguins found it hard to win. They still weren't a very good defensive team and they couldn't seem to find a goalie who could stop the other team from scoring. Lots of offense was entertaining, but championship teams have to play defense, too. Before the 1988–89 season, they replaced their head coach again, hiring Gene Ubriaco, and Tony Esposito replaced Eddie Johnston as general manager, taking over the responsibility of acquiring players either through the draft or trade.

Lemieux and the Penguins got off to a quick start. In the first month of the season, Mario was virtually unstoppable, scoring an amazing 18 goals with 23 assists in the Penguins' first 12 games. Winger Rob Brown emerged to give the Penguins another scoring option, and the combination of goalies Wendell Young and Tom Barrasso, obtained in a trade in mid-November, gave the Penguins their best goaltending in years.

Although cooled off from his record-setting scoring pace, the Penguins continued to play well, winning 12 times and losing only once from late November to late December. For the first time since Lemieux joined the team, they were in first place.

By the All-Star Game in February, the Penguins were a virtual lock to make the playoffs. Lemieux responded with a tour-de-force performance in the game, collecting 3 assists and 3 goals, including the game winner in sudden-death overtime in the Prince of Wales Conference's 6–5 win.

Although the Penguins slumped for the next month, they came on strong at the end of the season to finish second in the division with a 40–33–7 record to qualify for the playoffs. Lemieux won another scoring title with an incredible 199 points, leading the league with 85 goals and tying Gretzky for the lead in assists with 114.

In the first round, they faced the New York Rangers. The Penguins dispatched the Rangers in 4 straight games, setting up a quarterfinal matchup against the Philadelphia Flyers, their arch rivals.

Until recently, the rivalry had been decidedly one-sided. From 1974 until earlier in the 1988–89 season, the Penguins hadn't won a game in Philadelphia, playing an incredible 41 games against the

Flyers on their home ice without a victory. But late in the season, they had finally broken through, beating the Flyers twice, including a thrilling overtime win in the last game of the season. Entering the series, the Penguins were confident.

It was a tough series. After the Penguins won Game Five by the incredible score of 10–7, they needed only 1 more victory to advance to the semifinals.

But in the playoffs, one player can make the difference. In Game Six, after starting Philadelphia goalie Ron Hextall was injured, Ken Wregget came off the bench and played the best hockey of his career. He virtually shut down the Penguins, holding them to only 1 goal in the seventh game while turning away 39 shots. The Flyers won the series. Lemieux had played well in his first taste of Stanley Cup action, scoring 19 points in 11 games, but it hadn't been quite enough. He and his teammates were determined to go deeper into the playoffs in the upcoming season.

They seemed well on their way to a return engagement in the playoffs during the 1989–90 season. After a slow start, Craig Patrick took over as coach and general manager, and the Penguins responded. Lemieux, in particular, was a picture of consistency. From October 31 thru February 11, he scored in 46 straight games, the second longest streak in NHL history, highlighted by his performance in the All-Star Game played in Pittsburgh. Before the home crowd, he scored 4 goals and won his third All-Star Game MVP award.

But the game everyone remembered that year was played on February 14 versus the Rangers. Lemieux suffered a serious injury, a herniated disk in his back that made it painful for him to move at all, much less skate or take the pounding of playing hockey. Although hockey fans joked that his back had given out because he had been carrying the Penguins for so long, such injuries can be career threatening.

Lemieux rested his back and took physical therapy, trying to avoid surgery. He hoped to return and play for the Penguins in the playoffs. But with Lemieux out, the Penguins went into a terrible slide, winning only 5 games in his absence.

With 1 game left in the season, the Penguins needed a win to make the playoffs. Lemieux announced that he would try to play in the season finale against the Buffalo Sabres at the Igloo.

As one writer noted, "He didn't come back because he was cured. Or even homesick. Lemieux made the trip because the Penguins had one game left and needed at least a tie to clinch a playoff spot." The home crowd greeted him with a huge roar when he took the ice in pregame warm-ups, but soon after the game started it was clear that Lemieux was still bothered by the injury. Despite playing at what one teammate estimated as about 25 percent of his ability, he still managed to score 1 goal and set up another. Inspired by his return, the Penguins played hard and took the game into overtime. But the Sabres slipped in a goal to win the game, and the Penguins missed qualifying for the playoffs by a single point.

Lemieux and his teammates were disappointed but were already looking ahead to the 1990–91 season. Lemieux had spent several months waiting for his back to heal on its own, but once it became apparent it would not, he underwent surgery in mid-

Mario Lemieux jumps for joy after making his first NHL goal, in a game against the Boston Bruins.

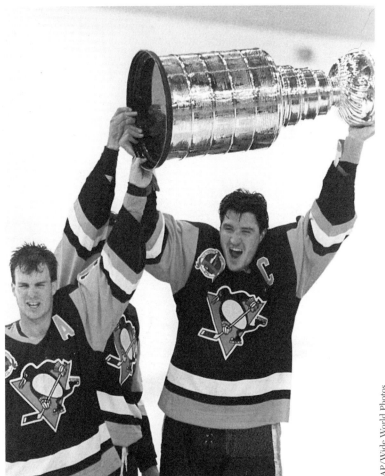

Lemieux hoists the coveted Stanley Cup above his head after the Penguins' 1991 victory over the Minnesota North Stars.

A full body slam from a Florida Panther sends Lemieux flying backward.

Lemieux, right, and his teammate Jaromir Jagr share a laugh before a game against the Boston Bruins.

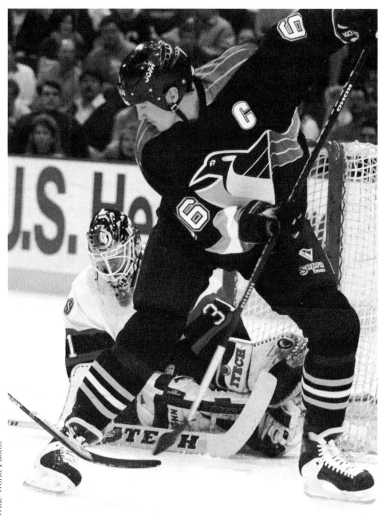

With a deft shot between his legs, Lemieux shows one of the moves that earned him the nickname Super Mario.

Sending ice chips flying, Lemieux slides into the goal in a determined attempt to put the puck past the Vancouver Canucks goalie.

Poetry in motion, Lemieux flies down the ice with the puck.

Lemieux and Jagr tap gloves in celebration of a goal.

Mario Lemieux's Career Stats

Year	Team	GP	Games	A	TP	PIM	+/-	PP	SH	GW	GT	Shots	Pct
84-85	Penguins	73	43	57	100	54	-35	11	0	2	0	209	20.6
85-86	Penguins	79	48	93	141	43	-6	17	0	4	0	276	17.4
86-87	Penguins	63	54	53	107	57	13	19	0	4	0	267	20.2
87-88	Penguins	77	70	98	168	92	23	22	10	7	0	382	18.3
88-89	Penguins	76	85	114	199	100	41	31	13	8	0	313	27.2
89-90	Penguins	59	45	78	123	78	-18	14	3	4	0	226	19.9
90-91	Penguins	26	19	26	45	30	8	6	1	2	0	89	21.3
91-92	Penguins	64	44	87	131	94	27	12	4	5	0	249	17.7
92-93	Penguins	60	69	91	160	38	55	16	6	10	0	286	24.1
93-94	Penguins	22	17	20	37	32	-2	7	0	4	0	92	18.5
95-96	Penguins	70	69	92	161	54	10	31	8	8	0	338	20.4
96-97	Penguins	76	50	72	122	65	27	15	3	7	0	327	15.3
00-01	Penguins	43	35	41	76	18	15	16	1	5	0	171	20.5
01-02	Penguins	11	1	9	10	4	-3	0	0	0	0	42	2.38
Totals		799	649	931	1580	759	155	217	49	70	0	3267	19.9

Mario Lemieux's Playoff Stats

Year	Team	GP	Games	A	TP	PIM	+/-	PP	SH	GW	GT	Shots	Pct
88-89	Penguins	11	12	7	19	16	-1	7	1	0	0	41	29.3
90-91	Penguins	23	16	28	44	16	14	6	2	0	0	93	17.2
91-92	Penguins	15	16	18	34	2	6	8	2	5	0	69	23.2
92-93	Penguins	11	8	10	18	10	2	3	1	1	0	40	20
93-94	Penguins	6	4	3	7	2	-4	1	0	0	0	23	17.4
95-96	Penguins	18	11	16	27	33	3	3	1	2	0	78	14.1
96-97	Penguins	5	3	3	6	4	-4	0	0	0	0	19	15.8
00-01	Penguins	18	6	11	17	4	4	1	0	3	0	39	15.4
Totals		107	76	96	172	87	20	29	7	11	0	402	18.9

Mario Lemieux's Career Highlights

1984-85:
Awarded Calder Memorial Trophy

1985-86:
Member of the All-Star Team
Winner of the Lester B. Pearson Award

1986-87:
Member of the All-Star Team

1987-88:
Member of the All-Star Team
Winner of the Art Ross Trophy
Winner of the Hart Memorial Trophy
Winner of the Lester B. Pearson Award

1988-89:
Member of the All-Star Team
Winner of the Art Ross Trophy

1990-91:
Winner of the Conn Smythe Trophy

1991-92:
Member of the All-Star Team
Winner of the Art Ross Trophy
Winner of the Conn Smythe Trophy

1992-93:
Member of the All-Star Team
Winner of the Art Ross Trophy
Winner of the Hart Memorial Trophy
Winner of the Lester B. Pearson Award
Winner of the Bill Masterson Memorial Award

1995-6:
Member of the All-Star Team
Winner of the Art Ross Trophy
Winner of the Hart Memorial Trophy
Winner of the Lester B. Pearson Award

1996-97:
Member of the All-Star Team
Winner of the Art Ross Trophy

1999:
Becomes part owner of the Pittsburgh Penguins

2000-01:
Comes out of retirement to play for the Penguins
Winner of the Lester Patrick Trophy
Captain of the All-Star Team

2001-02:
Olympic gold medalist (played for Canada)

July so he would be ready to return in the upcoming season.

In the meantime, general manager and coach Craig Patrick got busy. After watching the team for a season, he concluded that he knew what they needed and decided to focus his efforts on the general manager's job. He resigned as coach and hired Bob Johnson, an enthusiastic, defensive-minded coach who had enjoyed success at both the University of Wisconsin and with the Calgary Flames.

The loss of Lemieux had exposed the Penguins as one-dimensional. Craig Patrick was determined to surround Lemieux with better players. He made several important trades and picked up winger Jaromir Jagr in the draft. The young Czechoslovakian player, while lacking Lemieux's passing and playmaking skills, was a bona fide goal scorer. The opposition wouldn't be able to focus all their efforts defending against Mario with Jagr playing on the same line as Lemieux. If they did — or if Lemieux was out with an injury — Jagr could still put the puck into the net.

The Penguins started training camp enthusiastically. Jagr and the other new players gave the team more talent than ever before, and the team responded to Johnson's style of coaching. According to Johnson, every day was "a great day for hockey." His players fed off his passion for the game.

But just a couple weeks before the start of the regular season, Lemieux began experiencing pain in his back again. He was initially mystified because the pain was different than what he had experienced from the herniated disk. At first, he tried to play through it, thinking it was just a normal reaction as his body healed and his back recovered, but he soon had to leave the ice.

Team doctors diagnosed Lemieux with an infection that was unrelated to either the disk injury or the surgery. "This is a very uncommon thing," said one doctor. "The good news is that this is a treatable problem. We can make it go away. He needs antibiotics and total rest." It was unlikely he'd be able to return to the lineup until the middle of the season.

The Penguins tried to look on the bright side. "I'd rather have him for the second half than the first half," said Paul Coffey. "We'll try to get off to a good start," said Coach Johnson. "Sometime we're going to get the best player in the league back."

The season would start with Mario Lemieux watching his teammates on television. He promised himself that he would end the season on the ice, hoisting the Stanley Cup over his head.

Chapter Seven:

1990–92

Raising the Cup

With Lemieux out of the lineup, no one expected much from the Penguins in the 1990–91 season. But the Penguins were determined to play well. In a way, his absence at the start of the season may have even helped them. Every player on the roster worked a little harder and tried to pick up the slack. While the rest of the league expected the Penguins to collapse, they proved surprisingly tough.

They made the most improvement on defense. Ever since Lemieux joined the team, the Penguins had usually won only when they scored big, collecting 5 or 6 goals. But when they experienced an off night and scored only 2 or 3 goals, the opposition usually outscored them and won. In the 1989–90 season, the Penguins had given up nearly 5 goals per game.

Coach Johnson knew that good defensive play was primarily the result of effort and concentration. Without Lemieux's scoring touch, the team just couldn't afford to relax and give away low-scoring games. They had to stay focused and work just as hard on defense as on offense.

The results were a little unexpected. As the Penguins' defense improved, so did their offense. The opposition had to work hard on both ends of the ice and never had a chance to take a breather and relax. As a result, they often became tired and found it difficult to defend the Penguins. Pittsburgh's offense responded to Lemieux's absence with a much more balanced attack that was surprisingly potent. A half-dozen players had the ability to jump on mistakes and score at any time. Jaromir Jagr was one of the best rookies in the league, and Mark Recchi blossomed into a full-fledged star.

Goalie Tom Barrasso was the Penguins' last line of defense. He became a solid goaltender and rarely gave up a score without making the other team work for it. The Penguins started the season fast, and while most observers expected them to tail off, they never did. As Lemieux began working out with the team to get back in shape and return to action, the Penguins surged, trailing the division-leading New York Rangers by only a few points. Pittsburgh fans, looking ahead to Lemieux's return, began to believe that the Penguins had a chance to win the Stanley Cup.

Lemieux returned to action on January 29 against the Quebec Nordiques in Quebec City. The press wondered if the Penguins might relax and stop working hard.

"I'd worry about that a lot more if everybody in this room hadn't been asked that so many times," said teammate Phil Bourque. "Keep asking. It's good for us."

They needn't have worried. The Penguins continued to display the same work ethic they had shown all year. Lemieux played up to his customary standard after the long layoff, picking up 3 assists in his return, and the Penguins won 6–5.

Three days later, the Penguins went into Washington to play the Capitals and quickly fell behind 2–0. But just before the end of the first period, Lemieux knocked the puck away from a Washington player to teammate Mark Recchi. Recchi immediately passed it back to Lemieux, and as the defense closed in, he hit Bob Erry with a perfect pass in the goalmouth to make the score 2–1.

Entering the third period, the Penguins still trailed. Lemieux reached out and stole another pass, tipping it to Jagr, who then passed the puck back to Lemieux. He slapped it into the net before the goaltender could react, tying the score. Pittsburgh went on to win!

Lemieux's teammates were impressed. "I can't believe a guy can be off that long and play like that," said Bourque. "It must be a great feeling to know you can take control of a game."

More than sixteen thousand Penguin fans — a full house — filled the arena to welcome Lemieux back for his first home game in eleven months. They waved signs that said simply "MARIO" and cheered him from the moment he stepped onto the ice. Coach Johnson knew that it would be an emotional experience for his team and warned them all before the game. "Don't get caught up in the show," he said. "Make sure you play the game."

The Penguins took Johnson's advice and in the second period took a comfortable lead. Then, as

Lemieux skated after the puck, he pulled up and had to return to the bench. He had pulled a groin muscle. Although the Penguins won 6–2, Lemieux had to sit out another week to allow the injury to heal.

Fortunately, when he came back he was able to resume his expected level of play, and the Penguins continued to play hard. With a month left in the season, Patrick engineered an important trade, acquiring rugged defenseman Ulf Samuelsson and veteran center Ron Francis to give the team some added depth and toughness. With Lemieux scoring nearly 2 points a game, the Penguins ended the season on a high note, winning 9 of their final 15 games and beating the Rangers in 2 late-season contests to edge them out of the Patrick Division title.

Winning the Division gave the Penguins a huge boost before entering the Stanley Cup playoffs. The team with the best regular season record had the home-ice advantage and a big edge in the playoffs.

The Penguins faced the New Jersey Devils in the first round and were put to the test, falling behind in the series 3 games to 2 before winning the last 2 games to advance. They then dumped the Washington Capitals, winning 4 straight games after losing the first game. If the Penguins defeated the Boston Bruins in the Prince of Wales Conference finals, they would play for the Stanley Cup.

The Penguins lost the first 2 games, then surged back, winning 4 in a row to reach the finals. If they could beat the surprising Minnesota North Stars, they would win the championship.

Both the Penguins and the North Stars had joined the NHL as expansion teams in 1968. Neither had won the Stanley Cup before. Furthermore, the matchup was the first finals in the history of the NHL that paired two teams from the United States. The winner was certain to make history.

Most observers thought that the North Stars were the better team in most areas of the game but admitted that the Penguins had a not-so-secret weapon that could make all the difference — Mario Lemieux. Lemieux had surpassed Gretzky as the best player in the NHL. But unlike Gretzky, he had yet to lead his team to a championship. That was the only thing missing on his hockey résumé.

The finals opened in Pittsburgh, but for the fourth straight series, the Penguins lost the first game.

Despite having a two-man advantage due to several penalties during the game, the North Stars were adept at killing penalties. North Stars goalie John Casey turned back a flurry of shots, and Minnesota escaped with a 5–4 win.

In Game Two, the Penguins took a quick 2–0 lead. But Minnesota roared back to score a goal and take the momentum from Pittsburgh. Then Lemieux took command and keyed a Penguin win with one of the most spectacular goals of his career.

After a delayed penalty call, in which play continues after a penalty until play is stopped, Lemieux went on the attack, scooping up the loose puck and carrying it through the neutral zone. Two Minnesota defenders met him at the blue line.

Had two defenders converged on any other player in the league, that player would probably have been knocked to the ice and lost control of the puck. But not Lemieux. He faked to the outside then cut back in between the two players. He kept control of the puck by using his backhand to slide the puck in between one of the defenders' legs.

While they scrambled to recover, Lemieux continued to control the puck. But as he careened toward the goal, he lost his balance. He started to fall to the ice at the crease, but on his way down he somehow managed to slide the puck from his forehand to his backhand. From his knees, he slipped the puck into the net, just wide of John Casey's skate! Goal! The Penguins led 3–1.

The Penguins swept to a 4–1 win to tie the series. The win proved critical, because Lemieux missed Game Three with back spasms due to sleeping on a too-soft mattress. Although the Penguins played well without him, Minnesota won to move ahead in the series.

Lemieux returned to action in Game Four and again proved to be the difference. The Penguins opened the game with a rush. When Lemieux scored only three minutes into the first period, the Penguins already led 3–0. They held on to tie the series at 2 games apiece.

In Game Five, Lemieux put the North Stars away early, grabbing a wide shot off the boards and again switching from his forehand to his backhand to score Pittsburgh's first goal. Then, with the

Penguins up 2–1, he hit Mark Recchi with a perfect pass for an assist as they increased their lead to 3–1. Although Minnesota came charging back, the Penguins held on to win 6–4 before their home crowd. They flew to Minnesota for Game Six, needing only one more victory to win the Stanley Cup.

Lemieux and the Penguins were determined to return to Pittsburgh with the Stanley Cup sitting in a first-class seat on the team plane. They wouldn't be denied.

The Penguins scored 3 first-period goals, including a shorthanded goal by Lemieux, to silence the crowd and put the North Stars on their heels. The Penguins then spent the last two periods celebrating and shutting down the North Stars. They scored 5 unanswered goals as Tom Barrasso stopped every Minnesota shot.

When the final whistle sounded, the Penguins swarmed the ice for the awarding of the Stanley Cup. Lemieux, who had scored at least 1 goal in each playoff game in which he participated, won the Conn Smythe Trophy, an award given to the MVP of the playoffs. As goalie Tom Barrasso said, "There wasn't going to be hockey in Pittsburgh anymore if not for Mario, and we wouldn't have won the Cup without him." Coach Bob Gainey of Minnesota concurred. "We were hoping Mario would just be regular," he said with a sigh. But he wasn't. He had been spectacular.

Winning the Conn Smythe Trophy was nice, but Lemieux enjoyed winning the Stanley Cup even more. When league officials carried the Cup onto the ice and awarded it to the Penguins, Lemieux, the team captain, grabbed the Cup with both hands and hoisted it over his head with a huge smile on his face. The Penguins were champions!

The Penguin celebration continued when the team returned to Pittsburgh. There is a tradition attached to winning the Stanley Cup. Every player on the winning team is allowed to have the trophy for a day. The Penguins allowed goalie Tom Barrasso to keep the trophy the first night, and he placed it on the front lawn of his Pittsburgh home for everyone to see. The next day he drove the trophy to Mario Lemieux's for a big team party.

Somehow — no one is quite sure how — the

Stanley Cup ended up on the bottom of Lemieux's pool. It took Lemieux and several teammates to dive down and carry it back to the surface. But they didn't mind. They wanted to make carrying the Cup a Penguin tradition.

Chapter Eight:
1991–92

Another Cup

The Penguins looked like an emerging dynasty. Lemieux was now considered the best player in the NHL. While Wayne Gretzky, in his prime, may have been a better player, at age thirty his performance was beginning to slip. Lemieux was nearing twenty-six years old and still improving. His troublesome back had held up.

The Penguins also seemed likely to improve. Jaromir Jagr looked like a future star, and Tom Barrasso had proven his value in the playoffs. The team loved playing for Bob Johnson. The Penguins were a near perfect blend of youth and experience, a team with a potent offense and an aggressive defense. Other NHL teams looked at the Penguins with envy, and Pittsburgh fans were optimistic about the future.

But the off-season revealed a host of problems. A number of players, among them Mark Recchi, Kevin Stevens, and Ron Francis, were free agents. After helping to bring Pittsburgh the Stanley Cup, they were looking for big raises for the 1991–92 season.

In reality, owner Eddie DeBartolo was overextended. While the Penguins were successful at the gate, Pittsburgh, compared to many other NHL cities, was small. Television and radio simply didn't provide as much revenue as broadcasting deals in other cities. The Penguins weren't broke, but they weren't making money either. There were rumors that DeBartolo, who also owned the NFL San Francisco 49ers, was looking to sell the team.

But even those problems were made to look insignificant on August 29. Just as the players were preparing for training camp, Coach Johnson was diagnosed with brain cancer and hospitalized. The prognosis wasn't good.

Johnson's illness rocked the Penguins. They began training camp under the direction of their assistant coaches, but nearly a dozen players were without contracts and didn't attend. Although Stevens and

Recchi soon signed new contracts, Ron Francis remained a holdout. Less than six months after winning the Stanley Cup, the Penguins were in disarray.

The club was hesitant to replace Coach Johnson, but as the season approached, they had no choice, due to his illness. Penguins director of player development Scotty Bowman, who had become a legend as the coach of the Canadiens, reluctantly assumed command on October 2, just a few days before the start of the season.

While the club opened the season by winning 4 of their first 6 games, and Lemieux was still the best player in the league, the team soon stumbled. Ron Francis returned in late October, but around that same time, Lemieux was forced to miss several games when his back started acting up again. The Penguins weren't playing like defending champions.

DeBartolo had made the decision to sell the team to Morris Belzberg and Howard Baldwin. While they waited for the sale to be approved by the league, there were rumors that the new owners planned to sell players to make the team profitable. Meanwhile, Coach Johnson's condition deteriorated.

The sale was finally approved on November 18. Eight days later, on November 26, Bob Johnson passed away.

Lemieux and his teammates responded with their best stretch of play all year, winning 12 of 16 games and thrusting the team into contention for the division lead. As 1991 turned into 1992, the Penguins seemed poised to march back into the Stanley Cup finals.

Then Lemieux's back started bothering him again. He'd been taking a pounding as the opposition focused their efforts on stopping him. Lemieux was frustrated by the constant rough play. After his back gave out on January 9 and knocked him from the lineup, he began to express fears about his future. He missed 9 of the next 14 games and admitted that he "thought about retiring." That announcement sent shock waves throughout the organization.

General manager Craig Patrick was determined to make some changes. The way the Penguins were playing, it was possible that they wouldn't even qualify for the playoffs, an embarrassing situation for the defending champs. He decided that he had to provide Lemieux with some protection.

In mid-February, he completed a complicated three-way trade with Los Angeles and Philadelphia, essentially trading Coffey and Recchi for Rick Tocchet. Tocchet, who played right wing, had the ability to score and to protect Lemieux. The Penguins were sacrificing some offense for size and defense, a strategy many Penguins disagreed with. Recchi was popular with his teammates and had scored a lot of key goals.

But Lemieux was thrilled with the acquisition. "Tocchet will be a great addition," he said. "Put Kevin Stevens on one side, Rick on the other . . . and let's go play hockey!"

It took a while for the team to adjust to the new lineup, and in late February, the Penguins finally started playing hockey, winning 11 of 14 games to secure a berth in the playoffs. The team appeared to be hitting stride at just the right time.

But on the precipice of the playoffs, the NHL players union went on strike. Although they quickly worked out their differences with the NHL owners, the ten-day layoff knocked the team off its stride. They finished third in the Patrick Division with a record of 39–32–9. The Washington Capitals had won the Division and were favored to dump the Penguins.

It didn't help matters that Lemieux was hurt again. At the end of the season, he injured his shoulder and missed the opener of the Penguins' first-round game against Washington. Pittsburgh lost and fell behind in the series.

They were down 2 games to 1 before Lemieux finally earned them a win. He played one of the greatest games in Stanley Cup history, netting 3 goals and collecting 3 assists as the Penguins won 6–5. But they failed to take advantage of the win and lost Game Four. They were 1 game away from being eliminated in the first round.

But Lemieux refused to lose. Coach Bowman changed the Penguins' defensive scheme. With their backs against the wall, Lemieux led the Penguins to 3 straight victories to defeat the Capitals in 7 games. "We were beaten by one man," said Washington coach Terry Murray afterward. "The difference? I'm just going to say this once. Number 66. Lemieux. Right now he's the best by far."

"I'm sure a lot of people were counting us out,"

said Lemieux. "We showed a lot of character coming back and winning the series." For the series, he collected 7 goals and 10 assists for 17 points, the third-highest total in NHL history in a seven-game series.

The victory earned the Penguins the right to play the New York Rangers in the next round. The Penguins won the first game easily 4–2, as Lemieux contributed 2 assists. "No one in the world is playing better now," said teammate Kevin Stevens.

The Rangers knew they would have to stop Lemieux to beat the Penguins. Only five minutes into Game Two, they did.

Ranger Adam Graves raised his stick and whacked Lemieux across the back of his left hand. Although his hand was protected by a glove, Lemieux immediately crumpled to the ice.

His left hand was broken. Team doctors told him he wouldn't be able to return to action for four to six weeks. It appeared as if Lemieux's season was over.

But the Penguins refused to give up. The team had fought back all year long and they weren't about to stop now. Graves was suspended for his infraction, and the inspired Penguins fought off the

Rangers in 6 games. Winger Jaromir Jagr, in particular, picked up the slack in Lemieux's absence. Pittsburgh fans began calling him Mario Jr.

Without Lemieux, few observers gave the Penguins much of a chance against the Boston Bruins. While Lemieux kept saying he hoped to return for the series, no one really believed him. After all, the series started less than two weeks after he'd broken his hand, and his doctors thought it would be at least a month before he could play.

Although the Penguins won the first game in overtime, the Bruins sensed that the effort had exhausted the team. Entering Game Two in Pittsburgh, they were confident of victory.

Then, incredibly, Mario Lemieux skated out onto the ice. His hand was still sore and swollen, but he had decided to play. As the crowd roared, the Bruins looked on in disbelief. "Right there the series changed," said Bruin coach Rick Bowness. "All of a sudden we were in awe." And the game hadn't even started yet.

When it did, Boston's sense of awe grew. Even though Coach Bowman expected Lemieux to play for about fifteen or twenty minutes at most, once the game began, Lemieux wouldn't come off the ice. He played double shifts for most of the game and led the Penguins to a 5–2 win, scoring 2 goals and picking up an assist. "Mario's so good, it's sickening," said teammate Kevin Stevens. "It's ridiculous."

It got even more ridiculous in Boston. In Game Three, Stevens collected a hat trick as Lemieux assisted on all 3 goals in a 5–1 Pittsburgh win. Then, as the Penguins swept the series, Lemieux provided an exclamation point.

With the Penguins shorthanded, Lemieux gathered the puck in the Bruins' end and swept around Boston forward Adam Oates. But Bruins defenseman Ray Bourque quickly moved up to stop him.

Bourque hardly even slowed Lemieux down. Mario gave Bourque a move that got him off balance, then slipped the puck between the defender's legs and charged straight at goalie Andy Moog. As soon as Moog dropped down, anticipating a low shot, Lemieux calmly flipped the puck in over his glove. On the Penguins' bench, backup goalie Ken Wregget watched the play open-mouthed. He couldn't believe Lemieux had gotten it past Moog. "I'm not good enough to play in this league," he said.

Bourque added, "Right now he [Lemieux] can do whatever he wants."

The 5–1 Game-Four win put the Penguins in the finals versus the Chicago Blackhawks. Hockey fans were excited about the matchup, which would pit Chicago, known for their defense and the spectacular goal play of goalie Ed Belfour, against Lemieux and the Penguins' high-powered offense. The Blackhawks were riding high, winners of a record 11 consecutive playoff games. Chicago fans were looking forward to their first Stanley Cup since 1961.

At first, it appeared as if the Blackhawks would win their twelfth game in a row. They swarmed over the Penguins and scored 3 unanswered goals in the first fourteen minutes of play. But the Penguins weathered the assault and tied the game 4–4 when Jagr scored with less than five minutes left to play.

In the game's final seconds, the Penguins were desperate to score. As Pittsburgh's home crowd roared, and the clock ticked down the final seconds of the game, Lemieux fired a shot on goal that Belfour rejected.

But he couldn't control the puck, and it floated

free. As Lemieux rocketed past, he reached out his stick and with one hand slapped the puck past Belfour. The Penguins won 5–4!

Chicago changed strategy in Game Two, benching their two most potent forwards in favor of more physical players, hoping to slow Lemieux. But it made little difference. Lemieux still scored twice, and the Penguins went up 2 games to none with a 3–1 win.

The Blackhawks hoped to turn things around in Chicago, but in Game Three, the Penguins turned the tables on their hosts. Kevin Stevens scored early. Goalie Tom Barrasso turned away all 27 shots he faced to record a rare 1–0 shutout. The Penguins were 1 game short of a second straight Stanley Cup.

Desperate, the Blackhawks took a different tack in Game Four. This time, they turned to an all-out offensive attack, hoping to outscore the Penguins. But the Penguins had the greatest scorer in the game.

The two teams each scored 3 goals in the opening period, but as the game went on, Lemieux wore down his opponent. Although he scored only 1 goal, he assisted on 2 others. With a final score of 6–5, the Penguins had won the Stanley Cup for the second time!

And for the second time, Lemieux won the Conn Smythe Trophy as Stanley Cup MVP. Typically, however, the team captain gave credit to others, telling the press, "I'd have given it [the award] to Tommy," referring to Pittsburgh goalie Tom Barrasso. Barrasso, who had nearly lost his daughter to cancer a year earlier, had played the best hockey of his career.

With their second straight championship, there seemed to be no way to stop the Penguins. They appeared able to overcome anything — the death of their coach, trades, and the occasional loss of Lemieux to injury. But for Lemieux and the Penguins, the greatest test of all was still to come.

Chapter Nine:
1992–93

Miracle on Ice

From the time the puck was dropped on the ice for the first face-off in the 1992–93 season, the Penguins appeared ready to collect their third-straight championship. Before the start of the season, the Penguins signed Lemieux to a lucrative long-term contract worth $42 million over seven years. He immediately began earning his salary, scoring goals in Pittsburgh's first 10 games. The Penguins jumped out to an 8–0–2 start.

Everyone was running out of words to describe Lemieux. Even his nicknames — Super Mario and Mario the Magnificent — didn't seem sufficient anymore. What made his accomplishments even more incredible was the deteriorating condition of his back. Although his herniated disk had been repaired, examination of his back had revealed a host of other problems. He was afflicted with something called spinal stenosis, a birth defect that caused a narrowing of his spinal canal. He also had a condition known as spondylolysis, a series of stress fractures of his vertebrae, or backbone. Added to those problems was arthritis. Most players wouldn't even be able to play with such injuries, much less be the best player in the world.

Lemieux was forced to take medication to control the pain, and before each game, he went through a regimen of stretching and other exercises to loosen up his back muscles. After the game, he would have to pack his back in ice.

But in early 1993, Lemieux's back problems became the least of his worries. On January 7, team doctor Charles Burke was giving Lemieux's back a routine examination when Lemieux mentioned that he had a small lump on his neck. He'd first noticed the lump more than a year earlier, but it hadn't bothered him. Over the last few weeks, though, he'd had a sore throat that wouldn't go away and his neck had been a little sore.

Burke examined the lump. It was a swollen lymph node. Lymph nodes often become inflamed when the body is fighting an infection, and Burke thought that Lemieux's sore throat might be the cause. But when Lemieux told him he'd had the lump for over a year, Burke was immediately alarmed. A simple infection wouldn't have caused swelling for such a long a period of time.

The next day, a surgeon removed the peanut-size lump for examination. Three days later, the doctors told Lemieux that he had Hodgkin's disease, a form of cancer.

"I could hardly drive home because of the tears," the usually stoic Lemieux said later. Seven years before, Lemieux had agreed to become the spokesperson of the Pittsburgh Cancer Institute after a cousin had died of Hodgkin's. Now he was a patient. When he left the doctor's office, he wondered if he would survive.

He was concerned about far more than hockey. He and his longtime fiancée, Nathalie, had finally decided to get married and have children. She was six months pregnant. Now, Lemieux wasn't sure that he would survive to see his child.

Over the course of the next several days, his doctors conducted more tests. Fortunately, Lemieux had a treatable form of the disease. Doctors told him that there was a 90–95 percent chance that he could be cured. Still, he was worried.

Lemieux held a press conference on January 15 to talk about his condition. "I faced a lot of battles since I was really young and I've always come out on top," he said. "I expect that will be the case with the disease."

His doctors explained that Lemieux would undergo weeks of radiation treatment, being blasted five times a week for as long as a minute. His doctor was optimistic, saying, "We do not feel this will affect his long-term health and is not career or life threatening." He believed Lemieux might be able to return to the ice by April.

Still, Lemieux cautioned Penguin fans not to expect too much. Although there was a chance he'd be able to return to play before the end of the season, he said, "First things first. . . . I'll be back when I'm one hundred percent cured."

The next two months were rough. Treatment had to be delayed while Lemieux recovered from a respiratory infection. Then he started radiation therapy.

Radiation caused some of his hair to fall out and left him fatigued. Some days, he wondered if he'd ever play again. Although he felt terrible, he tried to stay in shape.

Meanwhile, his teammates were determined not to let the season go to waste. Although they struggled in his absence, they still managed to win more than they lost.

Lemieux's treatments went well. He took the last treatment on the morning of March 2 and then, incredibly, returned to the ice later that day. Even more incredibly, when he returned, he showed no ill effects of the layoff. He was the best player in hockey again.

The Penguins surged through the last six weeks of the regular season. After Mario Lemieux returned, they were virtually unbeatable, winning 17 consecutive games, a streak that left the hockey world shaking its head in wonder. Despite missing 20 games, Lemieux still managed to lead the league in scoring. "I even thought about it during radiation," he admitted. "I was determined to come back and regain the lead." On March 18 and March 20, he scored 4 goals in back-to-back games.

Entering the playoffs, the Penguins were odds-on favorites to win another championship. But after sweeping the New Jersey Devils in the first round of the playoffs, Lemieux's back started acting up. The Rangers upset the Penguins in the second round. The Penguins and their fans were stunned.

A lot of observers blamed coach Scotty Bowman for the defeat. They thought the coach had ridden the team too hard during the 17-game winning streak, and in the playoffs, he had become too dependent on using the same two lines of players and not making use of the Penguins' substantial depth. They blamed Lemieux's back trouble on Bowman's strategy.

The Penguins fired Bowman, and Eddie Johnston moved down from the front office and took over as coach. He didn't make any drastic changes. The organization believed that the team already had enough talent on hand to make it back to the finals.

After all, they still had Mario Lemieux. Mario the Magnificent was now Mario the Miracle Man.

Chapter Ten:
1993-97

Final Decision?

In the off-season, Lemieux's back continued to give him trouble, a problem that might have been made worse by the cancer treatments, which left him weak. Although Lemieux had played well after his return, it had taken every ounce of his strength.

In July, he underwent another back operation, and this time, doctors cleared away scar tissue that they thought was responsible for all the soreness. He was determined to come back at full strength, and the Penguins opened the season without him as he rehabilitated his back.

But the 1993–94 season was a disaster for Lemieux. After missing the first 10 games, he returned to action but was soon forced back to the bench with more back trouble. After sitting out several more games, he tried to return but was forced out again.

Even when he didn't play, he was clearly bothered by his back. He couldn't bend over to tie his own shoes and even had a hard time picking up his infant daughter. The situation was hard on everyone. The Penguins didn't know if they could depend on Lemieux, and it was hard for them to find any consistency.

Lemieux played only 22 games during the regular season. He decided to focus on getting ready for the playoffs. The Penguins still won the Patrick Division but were upset in the first round by the Washington Capitals. Lemieux played all 6 games, but he wasn't enough to carry the Penguins into the next round.

He was frustrated. Unless his back got better, he didn't believe that it was right for him to play. His situation was further complicated when doctors discovered that he was suffering from anemia, a blood disorder that causes fatigue, stemming from the radiation treatments he received back in 1993.

Lemieux reluctantly announced that he would sit out the entire 1994–95 season and try to get healthy.

As his agent explained, "He doesn't want to be a 20–25 game player for the rest of his career."

His teammates understood. "He was struggling and sluggish last season," said Kevin Stevens. "Maybe a year off is what he needs. I'm for whatever is best for Mario." So were most Penguin fans.

Oddly enough, there was an NHL player strike at the beginning of the 1994–95 season, and the season didn't start until January. But Lemieux wasn't tempted to return early. He wanted to spend an entire year trying rehabilitation. If he couldn't return to his former high standards, he planned on retiring.

Playing hockey had always come easily to Lemieux. Although he had stayed in relatively good shape, in the off-season, he played a lot of golf instead of going to the gym. And for Lemieux, nutrition had meant skipping the French fries when he ordered a couple of hamburgers at a fast-food restaurant. Now he knew that if he ever wanted to play hockey again, he would have to change his lifestyle.

Lemieux hired a personal trainer and a physical therapist, and dedicated his year off to getting in the best shape of his life. Although he couldn't do anything to cure his back trouble, he could strengthen the muscles of his legs, back, and stomach to help his back handle the stresses of professional hockey. He spent hour after hour lifting weights, riding a stationary bike, and running on a treadmill. While he knew he would probably never be entirely pain-free, if there was a chance he could play hockey again, he wanted to give it his full effort.

The Penguins lost in the Stanley Cup semifinals in 1995. Soon afterward, everyone turned their attention to the question of whether or not Lemieux would return to the ice.

His rehabilitation had gone well, and in the summer of 1995, he announced that he would return to the game. He would play, but he also planned to play smarter. Whenever the Penguins played back-to-back games, Lemieux would sit out the second game to protect his back. And he also indicated that he'd skip the occasional long plane flight to the West Coast. At Lemieux's size, long plane trips were uncomfortable and sometimes bothered his back.

But the Penguin team he returned to was much different from the team that had won the Stanley

Cup. Hockey salaries had risen dramatically, and the Penguins couldn't afford to keep all of their veteran players. They had been forced to trade talented veterans, like Kevin Stevens and Ulf Samuelsson. Meanwhile, Jaromir Jagr had become a star.

Lemieux's back held up during training camp and he didn't miss a practice. When he took the ice for the first game of the season in Pittsburgh against Toronto, Penguin fans cheered him long and loud. Although he failed to score a goal, he collected 4 assists and helped the Penguins to an 8–3 win. "Mario is Mario," said Toronto coach Pat Burns afterward. He was still the best player in hockey.

His performance put him atop the NHL scoring list, and the Penguins were again one of the best teams in the league. Paired with Jagr, Lemieux and his teammate formed the best one-two scoring touch in the league. As the season went on, Lemieux was surprised to discover that he was virtually without pain and was able to play more often than he expected.

And he was still able to turn in virtuoso performances that left everyone in the arena shaking their heads in wonder. In February, during a game against the Canucks, he scored one of the most spectacular goals of his career.

As he took aim on goalie Kirk McLean, Canucks Martin Gelinas reached in and knocked the puck off his stick. As Mario skated forward, the puck slipped between his legs behind him.

Then Lemieux did something no one in hockey could ever recall seeing before. He reached back with his stick behind him, then flicked the puck from between his legs. It tumbled over the goalie's shoulder and into the net for a goal.

McLean couldn't believe it. "You don't mind being on a highlight film when it's a guy like him," said the goalie later.

Later in the season, Lemieux had perhaps his finest game as a pro. In a contest versus Wayne Gretzky and the St. Louis Blues, Lemieux exploded. He scored an incredible 5 goals and added 2 assists in the Penguins' 8–4 win. Led by Lemieux, who also led the league in scoring even though he played only 70 of 80 games, the Penguins won the division.

Lemieux badly wanted to add another Stanley Cup championship to his résumé. But despite his 27 points in 18 playoff games, Pittsburgh lost in the semifinals to Florida.

Lemieux stepped back during the off-season and took a look at both his hockey career and his life. On the ice, he had accomplished nearly everything he had set out to do. Off the ice, he and Nathalie were now the parents of three children. He had proven he could come back and play at his previous level, but he began to worry about the long-term effects on his back if he continued to play. As his children grew up, Lemieux wanted to be able to spend time with them and do all the things most fathers do with their children — play in the backyard, roughhouse, and even go skating.

He made the most difficult decision of his career. At age thirty-one, he decided that the 1996–97 season would be his last. "I won a couple of championships and a couple MVP awards, but there comes a point in time when you want to do something else in your life," he explained. "I have three kids and I want to spend more time with them."

At the beginning of the season, it appeared as if Lemieux had made the right decision. Although he played well, he was no longer the goal-scoring machine that he had been for much of his career. In the first 30 games of the season, he never scored more than 1 goal in a game. Lemieux even admitted to one reporter that, thus far in the season, he thought he had played well only twice.

But as the day of his retirement began to approach, Lemieux came alive. For the last half of the season, he was Super Mario again, scoring goals in bunches.

As the season wound down, fans throughout the NHL came out in droves to see Lemieux play for what they assumed would be the last time. On March 26, 1997, when he played his final game in Montreal, nearly twenty-two thousand fans turned out to see their hometown hero. Lemieux said good-bye in spectacular fashion, collecting 3 second-period assists and then, as the clock ticked down the game's final minutes, scoring 2 late goals to lift the crowd to its feet and keep it there. Canadiens coach Mario Tremblay accurately called it "a scenario à la Hollywood."

But Pittsburgh fans knew they'd have a chance to see Lemieux in the playoffs. Although the Penguins struggled to play .500 hockey, they still qualified for postseason play and faced the Philadelphia Flyers in the first round.

There would be no Hollywood ending in the playoffs. The Flyers took a quick 3-games-to-none lead in the series. When Lemieux took the ice for Game Four in Pittsburgh, most Penguin fans assumed they'd never see him play hockey again.

Lemieux was determined to go out a winner. The Penguins played their best hockey in weeks and led 3–1 midway through the third period. Then, from every corner of the rink, fans started chanting, "MAR-I-O, MAR-I-O." During a time-out with only two minutes left to play, the team showed a brief video highlight on the scoreboard that ended with one of Lemieux's patented goals.

When the game resumed, the fans got to see similar play live and in person. With only a minute left, Lemieux got the puck on a breakaway, rocketed down the ice, and slapped in a goal, sending the crowd into a frenzy. The Penguins won 4–1. The fans cheered their loudest for Mario. Most were certain they'd never see a player like Mario Lemieux again.

Chapter Eleven:
1997–2000

Back in the Game

Three nights later, the Flyers overpowered the Penguins to advance in the playoffs, end Pittsburgh's season, and apparently end Lemieux's career.

When his career ended, he held a host of NHL records. His 2.01 points-per-game average was the best in NHL history. And while the argument about who was the best NHL player in history can never be answered definitively, Lemieux left little doubt that he must be considered in that conversation.

He enjoyed being retired. Lemieux had never been particularly comfortable in the public eye, and he looked forward to being able to withdraw and live like a normal person.

And he was financially secure. Even though he retired, his lucrative contract with the Penguins remained in effect. He would still earn nearly $30 million before it expired. In addition, Lemieux picked up several million more each year in endorsements and other activities. For the most part, he did exactly what he said he was going to do: spend time with his family.

One measure of his remarkable ability is that, shortly after his retirement, the Hockey Hall of Fame announced that it would waive the normal three-year waiting period and induct Lemieux immediately. At the ceremony on November 17, he gave a brief speech and put off any suggestions that he might play again. Some Canadian fans were hoping that he'd come back and play in the 1998 Olympics, but Lemieux underlined the fact that he was retired.

The Penguins were a different team without Lemieux, and the NHL was a different league. Although Pittsburgh remained competitive, and Jaromir Jagr was one of the most exciting players in the game, interest in the team waned, and attendance slumped. Similarly, without a big star, interest in hockey was down all over the league. Pittsburgh co-owners Howard Baldwin and Roger Marino, who had purchased part of the team in 1997, began to argue over the direction and control of the franchise.

The end result was a franchise in turmoil. In 1997, the Penguins began to experience financial difficulties and missed a scheduled salary payment to Lemieux. He sued in order to get paid. In the meantime, Marino and Baldwin continued to argue. For a while, there was speculation that the team would be moved. Eventually, the team filed for bankruptcy.

When he had first joined the Penguins, Lemieux was given credit for saving the franchise. In 1998, he decided to do so again by putting together a group to buy the team.

There was probably no other person in Pittsburgh who could have put the deal together. But to many people, Lemieux *was* the Pittsburgh Penguins, and he was able to attract investors to the project. Lemieux presented his plan to the U.S. Bankruptcy Court. It was accepted in September of 1999. Mario Lemieux, hockey player, was now Mario Lemieux, hockey owner.

He was more than just a figurehead. As majority

owner and chairman of the board, his ideas and his bank account were on the line.

Observers were shocked that Lemieux proved so skilled in his new role. He knew that the recent controversy had cost the team some fans, and he was determined to get them back.

The cost of a ticket to an NHL game had risen out of the reach of many working families. But Lemieux knew that the future of the game depended on its ability to attract young fans to the sport. If a person didn't become a hockey fan as a youth, there was little chance he or she would become a fan as an adult.

One of the first things he did was create a family section in the arena. An adult could buy a ticket for $25 and bring kids to the game for only $10 apiece. Ideas like that started bringing the fans back to the Penguins.

Although the team had lost an incredible $13 million during the 1998–99 season, in 1999–2000, the team broke even. Their future in Pittsburgh was secure.

Once again, Mario Lemieux had saved hockey in Pittsburgh.

Chapter Twelve:
2000–02

Back Where He Belongs

Lemieux was excited to be around hockey again. He loved going to the arena every day, even if it now meant putting on a suit rather than a hockey jersey. But the more he was around the game, the more he felt the pull of the ice.

He'd stayed in shape since retirement, and after three years away from the game, his back hardly bothered him. His children were growing up and not quite so demanding of his time. They were constantly asking him about his NHL career. They had been too young when he retired to remember much. He still laced up the skates on occasion to keep in shape and found himself wondering if he could still play.

Although the Penguins had turned the corner financially, there was still work to do. And now that he was invested in the team, Lemieux wanted to do all he could to help his investment.

In October of 2000, Lemieux appeared in uniform with Jaromir Jagr in a promotional video. He finally found the urge to return irresistible.

At first, he worked out in secret, putting himself through drills and skating for hours, and then finally playing with some trusted friends. He wanted to make sure he could still play and that his back would hold up. He didn't want to return and embarrass himself.

In early December, word began to leak out that Lemieux was thinking about returning. Penguin fans immediately got excited and tried to guess when he might come back, buying tickets for games in midseason.

He made it official on December 8. "I missed the game and I missed the challenge of competing," he announced at a press conference. "I'm excited about the challenge." He began practicing with the Penguins again. And over the next two days, the Penguins sold more than ten thousand tickets.

Some of his younger teammates only knew him as an owner and a legend. They were a little bit wary about taking the ice with the man who signed their checks. But Lemieux's old teammates, like Jagr, welcomed him back with open arms. "He didn't retire because he couldn't play," reminded the winger. "He's still the man. . . . He didn't come back to be an average player. He believes this team could win the Stanley Cup."

Lemieux pushed himself in practice, making sure he was ready. He was soon convinced he was.

He returned to action on December 27 in Pittsburgh versus the Toronto Maple Leafs. It was the best Christmas present Penguin fans could have hoped for.

Thousands of fans stood outside the arena before the doors were opened at 6:00 P.M. Ten thousand fans poured into the stands just to watch Lemieux take part in the pregame skate. They started chanting his name right away, and even the players on the Maple Leafs skated over and welcomed him back to the game he loved.

But some observers had been critical of the decision. They didn't think there was any way he could come back after not playing for more than three years. They doubted he would be the best player in the game, or even one of the best. A lot of professional athletes had retired and tried to come back before, but few had ever approached their previous level of play. Lemieux was determined to prove them wrong.

The Penguins had retired his jersey several years before. So before the game began, Lemieux and his four-year-old son, Austin, went to center ice and lowered his jersey from the rafters. Then the Penguins showed a series of highlight films that had the crowd rocking. But they hadn't seen anything yet.

Lemieux took the opening face-off, and the Penguins controlled the puck. Number 66 took the puck and skated in behind the net. Jagr trailed him and cut into the crease.

Lemieux anticipated the move and fired a pass onto Jagr's stick. Jagr buried the puck in the net.

Goal! Only thirty-three seconds into the game, with his very first pass, Lemieux had helped his team score. He was still Super Mario!

In the second period, he proved it again. This time, Jagr fed Lemieux a pass from the slot. Lemieux fired the puck past Curtis Joseph and into the net. Goal!

"He played as if he never went away," said teammate Alexi Kovalev afterward. Even Lemieux seemed to agree. "The vision is there," he said of himself. "The hands are still there. I didn't have any trouble finding players and making decisions. I didn't come back to be ordinary."

One writer described him as a "chess master . . . thinking three or four moves ahead of everyone else." Calgary Flames defenseman Denis Gauthier, who watched Lemieux's return on television, put it even better. "The guy scores on his first shift in the league, the last shift before retiring, and sets up a goal on the first shift of his comeback. I'm sorry, but that isn't human."

Although the Penguins were playing barely .500 hockey without Lemieux, after he returned, they won 2 of 3 for the rest of the season. Despite playing only 43 games, he still finished fifth in the league in scoring and second in the league MVP race. The only player to outscore him after his return was Jagr.

His storybook return to the game would have been absolutely unbelievable if Lemieux had led the Penguins to the Stanley Cup championship. But not even Super Mario can conjure up such magic all the time. Although the Penguins played well, they lost in the quarterfinals.

Going into the 2001–02 season, Lemieux had two goals in mind. The first was to help his team to their third Stanley Cup. The second was to take a gold medal home in the 2002 Winter Olympics in Salt Lake City, Utah. This second goal was to surround him in controversy.

Lemieux was a member of the Pittsburgh Penguins. He made his home in Pennsylvania. Many fans hoped he would choose to play on Team U.S.A. in the Olympics.

But Lemieux is Canadian, not American. He chose country over residence and signed on with the Canadian Olympic team as their captain.

Pittsburgh fans felt betrayed. And although Lemieux continued to play for the Penguins, helping them rack up victories, he sat out enough games to make fans question his loyalty. Was Lemieux holding back, possibly hurting Pittsburgh's chances for a playoff run, so that he would be fresh for the Olympics?

Lemieux claimed that his reason for sitting out games was because of a nagging hip injury. He had

had arthroscopic surgery for the problem in October, but continued to be plagued by pain. He admitted that he was pacing himself for the Olympics, but that his NHL team was equally important to him.

"I want to bring Pittsburgh another Stanley Cup and bring Canada a gold medal," he said shortly before the start of the Olympics.

He would achieve one of those two goals soon enough.

Canada hadn't won an Olympic gold in men's ice hockey for fifty years. Hopes were riding high when Canada took to the ice against Sweden in the opening game of the tournament on Friday, February 15. But Sweden surprised Canada with a hard-checking "torpedo" offense. They beat Canada 5–2.

Two days after the loss, team coach and NHL Hall of Famer Wayne Gretzky made an announcement that sent Canadian fans further into the dumps. Mario Lemieux would sit out Sunday's game against Germany because of continued hip pain. Though Canada managed to beat Germany 3–2, most felt the team's performance was lackluster. Would Canada be able to pull itself together for the final?

Lemieux returned to the lineup for the game

against the Czech Republic two days later. He fired up his teammates and the fans by scoring the team's first two goals. The game ended in a 3–3 tie, but most felt the Canadians had improved dramatically. Fans began to hope again.

Their hopes turned stronger when Canada beat Finland 2–1 on Wednesday, February 20, launching them into the semifinals against Belarus. Belarus had surprised the hockey world by beating Sweden to earn their berth in the semifinals.

"We can't and won't take Belarus lightly," Lemieux said when asked about the upcoming match. They didn't. They trounced their opponent 7–1.

Meanwhile, the other semifinal match between Russia and the United States ended with a U.S. win. The gold medal game would pit Lemieux and Canada against his adopted country.

The U.S. scored first, electrifying their fans. But Canada was not to be denied. With five minutes left to go in the first period, Canadian defenseman Chris Pronger fired a pass to Lemieux. Lemieux drew on his years of experience and his inner instinct. He faked receiving the pass and going for a shot, thus drawing the defense to him. But instead of catching the puck on his stick, he let it slide through his legs to Paul Kariya. Kariya was wide open. He flipped a wrist shot past U.S. goalie Mike Richter.

Less than two minutes later, Canadian Jarome Iginla scored again, giving Canada a one-point lead. Lemieux nearly scored a third point, but the U.S. goalie made a miraculous save.

Team U.S.A. tied the score in the second period, but Canada soon took the lead again. Going into the third period, the score was Canada 3, U.S. 2.

Both teams battled hard, but in the end Canada was not to be denied. The team added two more goals in the third. The final score was 5–2. After fifty years, Canada was finally bringing home the gold medal.

Lemieux and his teammates were overjoyed. "It was all worth it," Lemieux said later, meaning sitting out Pittsburgh games and withstanding criticism.

But his gold medal did not come without a price. Soon after the Olympics he was back on the ice with Pittsburgh. On February 26, he made his sixteen hundredth career assist in a losing effort against the Los Angeles Kings. It would be the last game of the season for him. On March 1, Super Mario let it be known that the pain in his hip was too severe for him to play the remaining 23 games of the season.

It is too soon to tell if Mario Lemieux will be returning to the game he loves at the start of the 2002–03 season. Few people would blame him if he decided to step down for good. After all, he would leave the game as the seventh highest scorer in NHL history, a six-time scoring champion, a three-time league MVP, and winner of two Stanley Cups, one Canada Cup, and an Olympic gold medal.

Still, Lemieux has surprised before. "I'd love to play, maybe until I'm forty," he said. If he does, fans can look forward to four more years of Super Mario.

Matt Christopher®

Sports Bio Bookshelf

Kobe Bryant

Terrell Davis

Julie Foudy

Jeff Gordon

Wayne Gretzky

Ken Griffey Jr.

Mia Hamm

Tony Hawk

Grant Hill

Derek Jeter

Randy Johnson

Michael Jordan

Mario Lemieux

Tara Lipinski

Mark McGwire

Greg Maddux

Hakeem Olajuwon

Alex Rodriguez

Briana Scurry

Sammy Sosa

Venus and
Serena Williams

Tiger Woods

Steve Young

The #1
Sports Series
for Kids

Read them all!

All available in paperback from Little, Brown and Company